Journey Begins

First Steps in Buddhist Practice

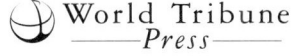
World Tribune
Press

© 2004 SGI-USA

Published by World Tribune Press
606 Wilshire Blvd.
Santa Monica, CA 90401

This booklet is based on an article that appeared in
the March 2003 *Living Buddhism*, which was compiled
from an article from the Soka Gakkai study journal,
The Daibyakurenge, June 2002, pp. 30–45.

Center cover photo © Kingmond Young
Left and Right cover photos © PhotoDisc
Cover and book interior design © Lightbourne, Inc.

Printed in the United States of America

10   9   8   7   6   5   4   3   2

Contents

The Journey Begins

People decide to practice Buddhism for any number of reasons—to cure a disease, find true love and success or to discover hope, confidence and meaning in their lives. Whether it is for these or for innumerable other reasons, ultimately people practice Buddhism to find true joy and fulfillment in life.

Now *you* have decided to practice Nichiren Buddhism. You've joined the millions of others around the world who daily use this practice to overcome their challenges, fulfill wishes and develop an indestructibly secure and happy state of life within. Congratulations and welcome.

To build this life of genuine happiness, you'll need a reliable foundation; so you'll want to know and master some basics. Based on Nichiren Daishonin's teaching, each of the points discussed in this pamphlet derive from practical experience. Millions of SGI members have proven that with these basic building blocks, anyone can construct lives of happiness for themselves and those around them. Take it from them, learning and practicing these basics throughout your lives is well worth the effort.

Each point here is discussed in very basic terms, but each plays an important role in your practice; they're simple but not simplistic. Please discuss them well with other members so you can genuinely make them a part of your lives. And return to them again and again throughout your practice to help keep yourself on track and to get the maximum benefit from Buddhism. For no matter how long you practice, the spirit to continually advance in faith and understanding will serve you well.

1

Seek Good Friends

We cannot practice Nichiren Buddhism alone. One of Shakyamuni Buddha's disciples once asked him: "Having good friends and practicing among them would be halfway to the mastery of the Buddha's Way, would it not?" Shakyamuni replied: "Having good friends does not constitute the midpoint to the Buddha's Way. Rather, it constitutes all of the Buddha's Way."

In Buddhism "good friends" in faith are people who lead you to and help you practice Buddhism correctly for the maximum benefit. Such good friends are important, Buddhism teaches, because in the course of our practice, obstacles and doubts will inevitably arise causing us, perhaps, to lose our original determination. Good friends can give us perspective, keep us focused on our goals and encourage us along the way of practice. Without such good friends, it would be difficult if not impossible to continue.

"The best way to attain Buddhahood," writes Nichiren Daishonin, "is to encounter a good friend. How far can our own wisdom take us? If we have even enough wisdom to distinguish hot from cold, we should seek out a good friend" (*The Writings of Nichiren Daishonin*, p. 598).

Fortunately for us, the SGI is a gathering of such good friends in faith. We support one another, pray together and offer timely encouragement and guidance. Staying in contact with other SGI members, especially when just starting out, is to our ultimate benefit. In fact, the path to happiness lies in seeking good friends and striving to become good friends ourselves.

2

Participate in Discussion Meetings

An SGI discussion meeting is a forum for life-to-life exchanges and an oasis of faith in the often harsh desert of modern life. At the meetings we gradually absorb the wisdom of Nichiren Buddhism and develop our faith. We may not always understand the topics under discussion, but our attendance will over time become an important cornerstone for faith and practice. While it is often difficult to find time to attend SGI activities, when we make the time for discussion meetings, we will certainly benefit.

Discussion meetings are a tradition dating back to the Soka Gakkai's birth in Japan. They embody the SGI's fundamental spirit of cherishing each person through heart-to-heart exchanges. By sharing our experiences and discussing Buddhism together, we contribute to one another's faith and gain immeasurable benefit.

The Soka Gakkai's first president, Tsunesaburo Makiguchi, initiated the tradition of discussion meetings in the 1930s. Rather than merely lecturing on difficult theories or concepts, he tried to communicate the greatness of Nichiren Buddhism by having members share their experiences of faith. He often traveled long distances just to attend discussion meetings and encourage each person there that they could become happy through faith.

The second president, Josei Toda, later stated: "You should come home from a discussion meeting feeling happy and inspired from having shared sincere conversation with fellow members—even with only one person or two. This is the kind of discussion meeting you should strive to hold— even if there is only one person who will listen to what you have to say. Just meeting with that one person is important."

Of course, the idea of individual believers encouraging one another stems from Nichiren Daishonin's teachings. As he once wrote: "All my disciples and followers should read and listen to this letter. Those who are serious in their resolve should discuss it with one another" (WND, 449).

An intellectual understanding of Nichiren Buddhism alone is not enough to propel our practice forward. Wonderful concepts can stimulate our minds, but it is the sincerity of another that can move our hearts. When both our minds and our hearts are engaged, we will feel motivated to take action. Sharing our experiences and realizations at discussion meetings—and listening to others do the same—helps us strengthen our resolve to chant and work harder for our dreams and goals. At the same time, as we encourage others who are going through hard times, we actually find ourselves encouraged and can thus awaken to a sense of mission to spread this Buddhism.

With laughter, moving testimonies and stimulating perspectives on Buddhism, our meetings help us to change fear into courage and inertia into action.

3

Attend the Buddhist
University of Life

Faith in Buddhism comes from experience and understanding. To experience benefit, we recite the sutra, chant Nam-myoho-renge-kyo and share the joy of practice with others. To understand Nichiren Buddhism and its profound teachings of life, it is crucial to engage in a lifelong process of Buddhist learning. As Nichiren Daishonin wrote, "Exert yourself in the two ways of practice and study. Without practice and study, there can be no Buddhism" (WND, 386).

Buddhist learning primarily involves reading and discussing Nichiren Daishonin's writings, supplemented by various periodicals and books that explore basic Buddhist concepts and the history of Buddhism. The SGI also sponsors many lectures and group study meetings in which we can explore with each other the critical points of Buddhist philosophy that will help us achieve breakthroughs in our lives.

The benefits of study are many. The more we study, the more confidence we gain in Buddhist philosophy, which in turns helps us deepen our faith, strengthen our practice and ultimately gain greater benefit. A deeper understanding also allows us to encourage and help others in their times of need. As we understand more about Buddhism, we also learn how to apply its teachings to our daily lives and can gain clearer insight into the workings of the world.

"Our foundation is Nichiren Daishonin's writings," writes SGI President Ikeda. "Studying them, we gain the courage to challenge injustice and the strength to build happiness."

Help Build an Ideal Community of Believers

The SGI, as a community of believers, has as its goal to help each person develop unshakable happiness, thereby realizing a peaceful society through the spread of Nichiren Daishonin's Buddhism. As one person's happiness inspires another, peace also spreads from one person to another. This is the reason the SGI focuses on individuals.

While people often associate religious communities or groups with restrictions on individuality and personal freedom, in the SGI we emphasize the ideal of "many in body, one in mind," a principle that harmonizes individuality with a common purpose.

In our SGI community, people are encouraged

to cultivate their unique qualities, an emphasis on diversity expressed as "many in body." We each share the same potential for Buddhahood and express it in our own unique ways. At the same time, we share a common goal—kosen-rufu, the widespread propagation of Buddhism that leads to a peaceful society. By staying focused on a common goal, expressed as "one in mind," we can create harmony despite our differences.

Of course, SGI members still have disagreements as well as personal likes and dislikes. Sometimes it is difficult to get along with other members or agree, for example, about the way activities should be conducted. With our diverse membership, this is natural. Herein lies the importance for each person to take responsibility for building the ideal community of believers that Nichiren Daishonin envisioned as "many in body, one in mind." Our Buddhist community empowers people to transcend self-interest so that they can respectfully disagree and still unite for the spread of Buddhism and for the realization of peace.

5

Establish a Consistent Practice

The prayer of Nichiren Buddhism—chanting Nam-myoho-renge-kyo and reciting essential portions of the Lotus Sutra—is an act of affirmation and praise of Buddhahood within our own lives and in the lives of all others. Our lives respond to this praise by manifesting Buddhahood—a life of courage, compassion, respect and wisdom.

Nichiren Daishonin wrote that chanting Nam-myoho-renge-kyo even once brings immense benefit. Unimaginable, then, is the benefit gained by those who recite the sutra and chant Nam-myoho-renge-kyo every day. For this reason, we shouldn't consider our practice as an obligation or do it out of force of habit. Our daily prayer is our right; a wonderful opportunity that allows us to uncover the precious gem of Buddhahood in the deepest recesses of life, thereby unlocking our truest selves.

Our daily practice is, in a sense, our "training for life" through which we can strengthen our lives from within. Consistency is most important. This is why we refer to our morning and evening prayers with the term *gongyo*, meaning "assiduous practice." With a refreshing morning gongyo we ensure the day's victory. With a sonorous evening prayer, we prepare ourselves for tomorrow's challenges.

While we can't transform our lives in a single day, through daily efforts over many years we can establish the state of Buddhahood as the foundation of our lives. We call this ideal practice "faith like flowing water," as opposed to a "faith like fire" that flares up at the beginning but soon "burns out."

Of course, circumstances don't always permit a twice-daily practice. If you don't have time to recite the sutra, you can simply chant Nam-myoho-renge-kyo three times. It is one's heart that is important, the desire to continue your practice throughout your lives. As Nichiren Daishonin states, "To accept is easy; to continue is difficult. But Buddhahood lies in continuing faith" (WND, 471).

6

Muster the Courage to Help Others

Our practice has two aspects: practice for oneself and for others. Personal practice is our daily prayer, and practice for others means helping them learn about or deepen their faith in Nichiren Daishonin's teachings, thereby empowering them to become happy. As a cart cannot move forward without two wheels, we cannot move forward in our Buddhist practice without both aspects.

Buddhism teaches the inseparability of self and others—that genuine happiness is not possible without helping those around us to enjoy their lives as well. By striving to share with others the happiness we get from our faith, we can build a self that can withstand anything life throws at us. Without such actions to help others, we may feel that something is missing in our own lives; but by reaching out to others in this way, we find ourselves enjoying the true richness of life.

Such compassion for others begins with the courage to transcend our own self-centeredness. Because it can be difficult to talk about Buddhism even with our closest friends, we need courage. Then we can invite them to discussion meetings or share our publications with them, wanting to communicate the greatness of the Gohonzon and the humanistic philosophy of Nichiren Daishonin's Buddhism. Ultimately, we realize that sharing Buddhism not only can benefit others but also aids in our own personal development.

The two aspects of our practice—for oneself and others—are inseparable. We cannot improve ourselves without developing the capacity to embrace others, and we cannot help others without strengthening ourselves. As we progress in our practice and study, we can better communicate about this Buddhism, with our behavior and attitude toward life being the most eloquent testimonies of all.

Of course, whether our friends start practicing is up to them. After all, faith cannot be forced, and in Nichiren Daishonin's Buddhism, which seeks to free the human spirit, coercion has no place. Regardless of our friend's decision, however, our efforts to share the Daishonin's Buddhism are worthy of respect and bring untold benefit.

Speaking about our efforts to share this Buddhism with others, President Ikeda once wrote: "For each of us, everything starts with developing connections with others, forging bonds of friendship and winning their trust." As we share our experiences in faith, communicating the greatness of Nichiren Daishonin's Buddhism through words and deeds, we expand our lives and inspire others to awaken their own supreme potential.

7

Strive for "Human Revolution"

Through practice, we will see positive changes in our circumstances, such as overcoming illnesses or improving our job situations. Although material or physical improvements are great, President Toda often explained that the true benefit of practice is the capacity to embrace life with joy no matter what happens.

The greatest benefit from our Buddhist practice is the unfolding of our Buddhahood, an inner strength that enables us to overcome anything, thus enabling us to enjoy each moment of our lives. We call the cultivation of this profound state of Buddhahood "human revolution."

Nichiren Daishonin states, "Benefit means to diminish evil and create good" (Gosho Zenshu, p. 762). Our lives are endowed with the ability to diminish life-negating functions that we would term *evil* and nurture life-affirming ones that promote *good*. This process of human revolution—the power to purify ourselves from within—is itself the greatest benefit of Buddhist practice. To this end, we chant, study and share Nichiren Daishonin's teachings and participate in various SGI activities. As we broaden and deepen our states of life, we experience great improvement, both spiritually and materially.

"As long as we maintain the determination to advance along the path of kosen-rufu," President Ikeda says, "adverse conditions will surely transform into benefit. You may not understand this right now. As time passes, however, you will look back and see that everything turned out well. It will become clear you have been advancing all along toward the fulfillment of your desires."

As we cultivate our innate Buddhahood and respect the potential for Buddhahood in others, we see positive changes in our lives, or benefits. On the other hand, if we deny ourselves or anybody else the path to Buddhahood, our lives become weak, confused and filled with suffering. Buddhism calls this "loss."

It is important to keep in mind that benefit or

loss is simply a reflection of our lives. In other words, benefit or loss is not reward or retribution received from outside forces. Nichiren Daishonin taught that we are responsible for both positive and negative aspects of our lives and that we have the innate power to create benefit and diminish loss. For this reason, it is all the more important to strive to bring about our own human revolution.

Experience Faith
Manifesting in Daily Life

Nichiren Daishonin's Buddhism is rooted in reality and stresses the inseparability between faith and daily life. Whatever our roles in life—parents or partners, workers or students—faith enables us to fulfill those roles to the utmost, solving the inevitable problems that arise and finding the greatest joy. The more we apply our Buddhist practice to our everyday situations, the more we discover how powerful a faith this is.

We are not Buddhists only when we are praying or attending meetings. Buddhism has the most value for us when we learn to apply the inner strength, wisdom and compassion we gain from our practice to help us succeed at home and at work. Those who neglect responsibilities and avoid challenges in their families, jobs or communities misunderstand the whole point of faith. True faith manifests itself in our daily activities, making our homes, schools and offices the very places in which the Daishonin's teaching of humanism and compassion can shine.

Other misunderstanding can arise, too, wherein we may even use faith as an excuse for inaction or as an escape from harsh realities. To take an easygoing attitude—"I'm chanting, so the Gohonzon will take care of all my problems"—is not faith but irresponsibility. Likewise, causing others to suffer, thinking "I can do whatever I want because I chant," is nothing but arrogance.

This faith of winning in our daily lives also requires concrete action on our part. We need both, for action without prayer is like a spinning wheel going nowhere, while prayer without action is mere wishful thinking. Buddhism is reason. If our prayers are truly in earnest, they will definitely give rise to action, and prayer coupled with action will bring about the fulfillment of all our desires.

9

Sustain Selfless Dedication

For the sake of people's happiness, Nichiren Daishonin dedicated his life to the spread of Buddhism. "From the time that I was born until today," he once wrote, "I have never known a moment's ease; I have thought only of propagating the daimoku of the Lotus Sutra" (WND, 965). Here "daimoku," meaning "title," refers to Nam-myoho-renge-kyo.

Propagating the teachings isn't just his mission, though. It's an integral part of everyone's Buddhist practice. "You must not only persevere yourself," he writes, "you must also teach others . . . Teach others to the best of your ability, even if it is only a single sentence or phrase" (WND, 386).

When we try to teach others, however, we too may meet with criticism, just as Nichiren did. In the early days of the Soka Gakkai, enthusiastic about their new faith, members shared this Buddhism with others, even though they themselves still had grave personal problems. As a result, they were often ridiculed. But they didn't wait till they had some external "proof," like more money or a bigger house. No matter how sick or poor, these pioneering members shared the Daishonin's teachings as a means to create fortune for themselves and to lead friends and family to happier lives in the aftermath of World War II. The real proof of their faith was their indomitable spirit to care for others despite the hardship.

The purpose of religion is to build happiness. No matter the struggle, the Soka Gakkai has always worked to fulfill this purpose. During World War II, Makiguchi and Toda were arrested for their adamant rejection of State Shinto. In contrast, the Nichiren Shoshu priesthood, fearing persecution, compromised their faith. Makiguchi and Toda maintained their beliefs in the midst of such extreme circumstances, continuing to express their religious convictions even to their guards and interrogators.

The SGI's spiritual roots are found in such selfless dedication.

10

Overcome Obstacles

As we practice Nichiren Buddhism toward accomplishing our goals, we will inevitably experience impediments to our progress. Nichiren Daishonin quotes sixth-century Chinese Buddhist scholar T'ien-t'ai: "As practice progresses and understanding grows, the three obstacles and four devils emerge in confusing form, vying with one another to interfere . . . One should be neither influenced nor frightened by them. If one falls under their influence, one will be led into the paths of evil. If one is frightened by them, one will be prevented from practicing the correct teaching" (WND, 501). He adds, "This statement not only applies to me, but also is a guide for my followers. Reverently make this teaching your own, and transmit it as an axiom of faith for future generations" (WND, 501).

In T'ien-t'ai's passage, "the three obstacles and four devils" refers to various obstacles and hindrances to our Buddhist practice, both internal and external. The faster a ship sails, the greater the opposing force of the wind and water. Likewise, when we practice to bring forth our Buddhahood, our lives experience resistance both within and without.

Obstructions, however, may not always seem negative. As T'ien-t'ai expressed, obstacles to our happiness appear "in confusing form." Some appear favorable yet nonetheless serve to undermine our Buddhist practice. Herein lies the most important reason to study Buddhism, so that we can develop the wisdom to discern the true nature of any circumstance. And as we practice, we develop the courage to stand up to obstacles as they appear.

When the Daishonin was exiled for the second time after a failed execution attempt, most of his disciples renounced their faith due to the shogunate's continual harassment. When the Japanese military government imprisoned Soka Gakkai leaders during World War II because of the organization's rejection of State Shinto, all except Makiguchi and Toda gave up their faith. But the ultimate victories of these men's lives demonstrate that developing wisdom and courage through practice allows us to overcome even seemingly insurmountable obstacles.

Buddhism teaches that becoming happy is synonymous with overcoming impediments to our happiness. We may still have problems, as everyone does, but from the perspective of Nichiren Daishonin's Buddhism, any obstacle we encounter in the course of our practice demonstrates our progress, becoming an opportunity to further develop ourselves. This is why the Daishonin warns: "Something uncommon also occurs when an ordinary person attains Buddhahood. At such a time, the three obstacles and four devils will invariably appear, and the wise will rejoice while the foolish will retreat" (WND, 637).

11

Challenge "Fundamental Darkness" Everywhere

All lives are equally precious. Nichiren Daishonin's teachings especially value the equality and sanctity of life: he declared that everyone possesses the potential for Buddhahood, a life of absolute happiness and the power to lead others to happiness as well. In other words, each person is important not only to him- or herself but also to the entire planet.

Intellectual understanding of this principle alone, however, does not automatically translate into self-respect, let alone respect of other people. Our lives are also imbued with what Buddhism calls "fundamental darkness," deep-seated human delusion that prevents us from seeing the Buddha nature in all life. This delusion provokes us into taking advantage of others for our own selfish ends.

Just as we cannot attain genuine happiness without overcoming obstacles, we cannot unveil our enlightenment without facing this fundamental darkness. We practice Buddhism to do just that, to win the struggle between enlightenment and delusion, to defeat our fundamental darkness and to protect human dignity.

Fundamental darkness often manifests itself in authoritarian tendencies. When we try to bend others to our will, we are not respecting their inherent Buddha nature. Conversely, when we bow in obeisance to others, we aren't respecting ourselves. Everyone has both positive and negative aspects, so while it is important to resist those who try to exert control over us, we must also reflect on our own negative tendencies.

The Lotus Sutra describes religious leaders who succumb to fundamental darkness and misuse their influence as "despising and looking down on all humankind" (*The Lotus Sutra*, p. 193). The sutra encourages its practitioners to challenge corrupt religious authority by repeatedly declaring that all people inherently possess Buddhahood (LS, 192–95).

Since its inception in the early twentieth century, the Soka Gakkai had been affiliated with the Nichiren Shoshu school of Buddhism, with its centuries old temples and priestly traditions. As has happened in many other religious traditions, there had been occasional tensions between priesthood and laity for decades. A defining event occurred in November 1991, when the Nichiren Shoshu high priest excommunicated the entire SGI lay association, effectively banning some twelve million members from participation in religious activities sponsored by the school.

The conflict stems from the priesthood's claim that the lay organization must submit to the absolute authority of the high priest and, further, to the superiority of the priesthood as interpreter of Nichiren's teachings. This, we believe, goes against the basic egalitarian spirit of Nichiren's teaching, which urges priests and lay believers alike to work compassionately for the happiness of all humankind. Instead, the priesthood has adopted an insular doctrine of priestly heritage in order to secure an authoritarian, clerical control over the religious practice and activities of all lay believers.

Genuine tolerance for people is based on steadfast intolerance of any disrespect for life. But to challenge those "despising and looking down on all humankind" we need honest and courageous self-reflection, because we possess the same tendencies, no matter how latent. Only through challenging the fundamental darkness both in ourselves and in corrupt authorities can we truly reveal our innate Buddhahood.

12

Awaken to a Sense of Mission

How often do we ask ourselves, "Why am I here?" With busy daily lives, thinking about the meaning of life may seem irrelevant or the luxury of idle philosophers. Even so, many people dread the possibility that their lives may have no purpose. So they look for someone or something to live for, thinking that a life lived for any purpose is better than living for nothing.

What purpose will bring us the most happiness? "To do, create or contribute something that benefits others, society and ourselves," says SGI President Ikeda, "and to dedicate ourselves as long as we live to that challenge—that is a life of true satisfaction, a life of value. It is a humanistic and lofty way to live." The purpose of our faith is to establish absolute happiness in this lifetime and beyond, for all eternity. For such lasting happiness to come, Nichiren Daishonin explains that we must fulfill our ultimate mission as human beings, our mission as Bodhisattvas of the Earth.

Bodhisattvas of the Earth appear in the Lotus Sutra. Shakyamuni entrusts them with the mission of spreading the Law far into the future for the sake of all living beings in the universe. Nichiren often identified himself as the leader of the Bodhisattvas of the Earth, and he urged his disciples to recognize their true identities, too: "If you are of the same mind as Nichiren, you must be a Bodhisattva of the Earth" (WND, 385).

Bodhisattvas of the Earth are not gods descending from the heaven. Their emergence from the earth signifies that they are ordinary people firmly grounded in the realities of life. The sutra describes them as having various splendid abilities, great wisdom and the will to endure all manner of difficulties in their desire to prove the greatness of the Mystic Law. All of us are Bodhisattvas of the Earth, and we fulfill this mission as we show victorious proof of our faith and share this practice with others.

While in prison during World War II, President

Toda awakened to his mission as a Bodhisattva of the Earth and practiced with "the same mind as Nichiren." In the early days, Japanese society criticized the Soka Gakkai as "a gathering of the poor and sick." But Toda told the members that they were Bodhisattvas of the Earth exactly as described in the Lotus Sutra. He held the conviction that Soka Gakkai members were not only the Buddha's envoys but direct disciples of Nichiren Daishonin. When we maintain "the same mind as Nichiren" to work for the peace and happiness of all people, our lives take on a richness and strength we did not know before. We gain unbounded energy and lose all fears. With a profound sense of mission as Bodhisattvas of the Earth, we can broaden our lives infinitely, thereby causing the ripples of peace to spread.

While we all have various roles to play in life, when we awaken to our essential identities as Bodhisattvas of the Earth, our lives, in all their uniqueness, take on an even more profound significance as models of hope and courage.

13

Learn from a Role Model

In his treatise, "Conversation between a Sage and an Unenlightened Man," Nichiren Daishonin states, "Both the teacher who expounds the principles of the Lotus Sutra and the disciple who receives his teachings will, in no long time, together become Buddhas through the power of the Lotus Sutra" (WND, 133).

The concept of teacher, or mentor, and disciple plays a crucial role in our Buddhist practice. Mentors prove the greatness of Buddhism through their own actions and are models of devotion to the spread of Buddhism. Disciples strive to learn the essential teachings of Buddhism from their mentors as they, too, work toward the shared goal of peace and happiness. Through their dedicated efforts, disciples actually live Buddhism instead of merely studying it as an intellectual concept. A genuine relationship between mentor and disciple, therefore, enlivens Buddhism practice. In its absence, Buddhism loses its grip on reality and deteriorates into formality.

The relationship of mentor and disciple isn't a formal or esoteric practice. Rather, it provides a way for disciples to learn how to practice Buddhism from a mentor's example. Such a relationship is not hierarchical or a means of control or coercive obedience built on loyalty and obligation.

In the Daishonin's Buddhism, mentor and disciple stand on absolutely equal footing, sharing the same goal of disseminating the correct Buddhist practice. The mentor values the disciple's potential while the disciple, inspired by the mentor's example, gains confidence in his or her innate Buddhahood. For this reason, the success of such a relationship primarily develops through the disciple's self-awareness.

The way of mentor and disciple has nothing to do with status in society or position in the Buddhist community. The connection between mentor and disciple is not determined by physical proximity. Instead, a disciple's vow to spread the

Law and contribute to the happiness of others in ways true to themselves is the key to the relationship.

Because the three founding presidents—Makiguchi, Toda and Ikeda—were keenly aware of the importance of mentor and disciple, they spread Buddhism on an unprecedented scale, thus enabling millions of people to lead lives of supreme happiness. From their examples we can learn the essential spirit and practice of Nichiren Buddhism and, through sharing their commitment to humanity's peace and happiness, develop our own supreme potential for Buddhahood.

SUGGESTED READING

For further information on Nichiren Daishonin's Buddhism, we recommend the following books, among many others. These books are available through any local SGI-USA community center bookstore, or from our Web site: **www.sgi-usa.org**

DOCTRINE

The Writings of Nichiren Daishonin

BUDDHIST HISTORY

The Living Buddha
Buddhism: The First Millennium
The Flower of Chinese Buddhism

HISTORY OF THE SOKA GAKKAI

The Human Revolution, box set

HISTORY OF THE SGI

The New Human Revolution (ongoing series)

Also, the following Middleway Press books are available through your favorite neighborhood or on-line bookstore, or at: **www.middlewaypress.org**

PLANETARY CITIZENSHIP

Your Values, Beliefs and Actions
Can Shape a Sustainable World

We also invite you to learn more about Nichiren Daishonin's Buddhism through our weekly newspaper, **World Tribune**, and monthly study magazine, **Living Buddhism: Journal for Peace, Culture and Education.**

Individual copies are available at: SGI-USA bookstores nationwide, or for subscription information please call: **(800) 835-4558** or go to **www.sgisubs.com**